Drawing Together to
Manage Anger

Written by Marge Eaton Heegaard

To be illustrated by children
to help families communicate and learn together

Published by Fairview Press, 2450 Riverside Avenue, Minneapolis, Minnesota 55454. Fairview Press is a division of Fairview Health Services, a community-focused health system affiliated with the University of Minnesota and providing a complete range of services, from the prevention of illness and injury to care for the most complex medical conditions. For a free current catalog of Fairview Press titles, please call toll-free 1-800-544-8207. Or visit our Web site at www.fairviewpress.org.

First printing: November 2003

Printed in Canada
08 07 06 05 04 03   7 6 5 4 3 2 1

Cover by Laurie Ingram Design (www.laurieingramdesign.com)
Interior by Dorie McClelland, Spring Book Design (www.springbookdesign.com)

We gratefully acknowledge the following experts for their assistance: Sharon Hearn, owner of Children's Book World, Los Angeles, California; Judy C. Wolfe, director of the Institute for Life Skills, Canton, Georgia; and Denise Giardina, program director of Youth Haven, Naples, Florida. And a big thank-you to Josh, Rico, James, Taylor, Timmy, Widline, Daniel, Arian, and Patrick for testing this book and offering great suggestions to make it better.

About this book

This book will help children and adults work together to understand and manager anger. It teaches healthy concepts while encouraging communication and bonding.

The book is designed for children ages six through twelve to illustrate with pictures they choose to draw. Younger children may need help understanding some of the words and concepts in this book, but do not offer too many suggestions. This is their book; encourage them to make their own decisions about what to draw or write.

Children like to illustrate books because images often come more naturally to them than words. I recommend that a child be given a small box of new crayons to draw with. While many children enjoy drawing with markers, crayons often encourage greater self-expression. Older children may prefer to use colored pencils and use words with their illustrations.

As you and the child work through the book together, focus on ideas and expression rather than drawing ability. The art process promotes self-awareness and communication, so invite the child to talk about his or her work.

When the book is completed, encourage the child to share his or her work with another adult for review and continued learning. Save the book as a keepsake of childhood memories.

This book can be used individually or with a group. Group facilitators should be supportive adults who are educated to accept feelings and encourage communication.

Adults can help children manage anger

Like adults, children suffer anxiety and stress. In addition to family crises—including illness, death, divorce, moving, and other life changes—children struggle with their self-esteem and sense of belonging. Many are teased or put down. They feel pressured to conform and succeed, and they often have a hard time accepting differences in themselves and others. When we add world terror, natural disasters, and adult personal problems, it's no wonder that children get angry.

Anger can be healthy. After all, everyone gets angry from time to time, and angry feelings are O.K. as long as they're expressed in appropriate ways. Many children, however, display explosive, violent anger, or they hold their feelings inside, thinking that anger is wrong or bad. Some children become angry when they don't get their way. Others use aggressive behavior to mask pain or fear related to abandonment, rejection, grief, loss, or depression. Unless these children learn to understand and manage their anger, they will cause unnecessary damage to themselves and others.

While children may learn some aggressive behaviors from friends, books, movies, TV, and video games, their primary influence is the family. Children learn how to express feelings by watching their parents. If parents do not express anger in positive ways, chances are their children won't, either.

This book can help families develop an awareness of anger-management problems and a commitment to change. Both children and adults are given an opportunity to learn how to calm their angry impulses while developing communication and problem-solving skills.

For example, parents must learn to be patient, express anger in direct and nonaggressive ways, and apologize for inappropriate behavior. Children should never have to witness adult rage or violent arguments. If it becomes necessary to punish a child, the punishment should always relate to the child's behavior, and it should be delivered in a calm and reasonable manner. Corporal punishment often causes children to rebel, which puts them at risk for delinquency when they are older.

When dealing with children's anger, adults can help children explore the roots of their feelings and learn to solve problems without aggression. Art, for example, is a safe outlet for angry feelings. It enables children to express emotions that are too difficult to put into words, and no one gets hurt. Encourage children to use the art process in this book, completing four of five pages at a time.

In addition to artwork, children can release stress through active play, exercise, and sports. Give them opportunities to gain positive recognition and increase self-esteem. Praise them when they find ways to use brain power instead of muscle power. And remember, some children—as well as some adults—have more problems managing anger than others. Don't hesitate to seek professional help.

This book is intended to help children:

To children

This is your book. You will make it different from all other books by drawing your own thoughts and feelings. You do not need any special skills to illustrate the pages. Just use lines, shapes, and colors to draw the pictures that come into your head as you read the words on each page.

Begin with the first page and do the pages in order. Ask an adult for help with words or pages you do not understand. When you have done a few pages, stop and share your work with an adult who cares about you.

I hope you will have fun with this book. As you share your thoughts and problems with others, you will learn to understand anger and develop healthy anger-management skills.

Adults get angry, children get angry,
and I get angry.

(Draw some angry people.)

Everyone feels angry at times. It is natural to feel
angry when you are afraid, or when you lose something
or someone important. Most anger is not violent or hard
to control, like the anger you see in movies or on TV.

1

People use different words for anger, like "mad," "furious," "annoyed," "irritated," and "ticked off."

(Write the words you use when you feel angry.)

You can feel a little or a lot of anger. These are normal feelings. Feelings are neither good nor bad.

Some people want to fight when they are angry. Children may want to hit, kick, bite, or yell.

(Draw what would happen if you were to hit, kick, bite, or yell.)

Unmanaged anger brings problems!

Some people want to run away when they are angry, or they try to hide their anger.

(Draw a picture of someone hiding their anger.)

Anger does not feel good, and many people hope it will just go away. But if anger stays stuffed inside, it can turn into depression. Or, it might build up to a big explosion of angry feelings.

Many things can bring an outburst of anger.

(Draw a volcano erupting.)

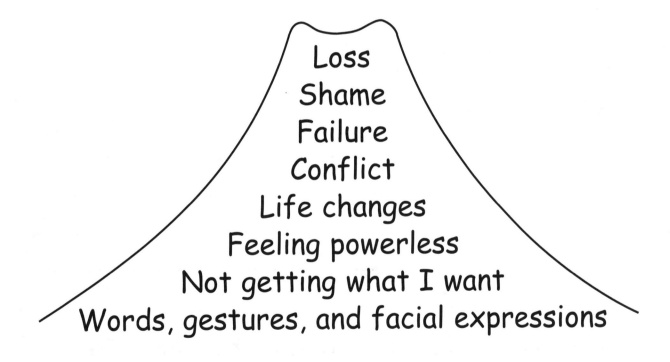

Loss
Shame
Failure
Conflict
Life changes
Feeling powerless
Not getting what I want
Words, gestures, and facial expressions

You can learn to let anger go without hurting yourself or others.

I get angry:

(Check ✓ what is true for you.)

never ____   sometimes ____   often ____

I am able to control my anger:

always ____   sometimes ____   never ____

Sometimes I get angry at _____
_____(name)
because_____
_____
_____.

Some people get angry more easily than others. They may get frustrated easily. Or they may have grown up in a family with poor anger-management skills. They have to work hard to manage their feelings and behaviors.

I know I am beginning to feel angry when:

(Check ✓ the things that happen to you.)

____ My breathing changes.
____ My muscles feel tight.
____ My heart begins to pound.
____ My body feels warm or shaky.
____ I clench my mouth, teeth, or fists.
____ I want to yell, kick, or hit.
____ I want to cry.
____ My head feels like it will explode.
____ Other: _____
____ Other: _____

As soon as you begin to feel angry, you can start to control it.

Many things can trigger feelings of anger. These are some of my triggers.

(Check those that have triggered your anger. Use one ✓ for "sometimes" and two ✓✓ for "often.")

____ Fear of danger.

____ Getting hurt.

____ Being teased or bullied.

____ Not getting what I want or need.

____ Pressure to succeed at home or school.

____ Loss of someone or something.

____ Not being allowed to do something.

____ Being told what to do.

____ Fear of standing up for myself.

____ Problems at home.

____ Verbal or physical abuse.

____ Being rejected by friends.

____ Thinking something isn't fair.

____ Not feeling loved or listened to.

____ Not doing something as well as I want.

When I am angry, I:

(Check ✓ the things you do most often.)

___ Just hope the feeling goes away.
___ Yell, kick, or hit.
___ Hurt someone.
___ Act as if I don't care.
___ Feel hurt and cry.
___ Count to 10 before I do anything.
___ Discuss the problem with the other person.
___ Talk about the problem with someone else.
___ Bang my head on the wall.
___ Say bad words.
___ Other: _____
___ Other: _____

Some people use anger to avoid hurting inside. But anger will not make your problems go away.

When I am angry, I feel the anger in my body.

(Close your eyes and think of a time you felt very angry. Use a red crayon to scribble the places where you felt your anger.)

Angry Feelings Inside	Angry Feelings Outside
	(Draw a picture of how you look when you are angry.)

Some people feel anger in their hands and feet (they want to hit and kick), in their mouth (they want to shout), in their stomach or head (they feel sick), in their heart (they want to cry), or in their brain (they think instead of feel).

Sometimes I hide my angry feelings by pretending to feel something else, almost like wearing a mask. When I am angry at a parent or teacher but am afraid to tell them, I put on this mask:

(Draw the face you use to hide angry feelings.)

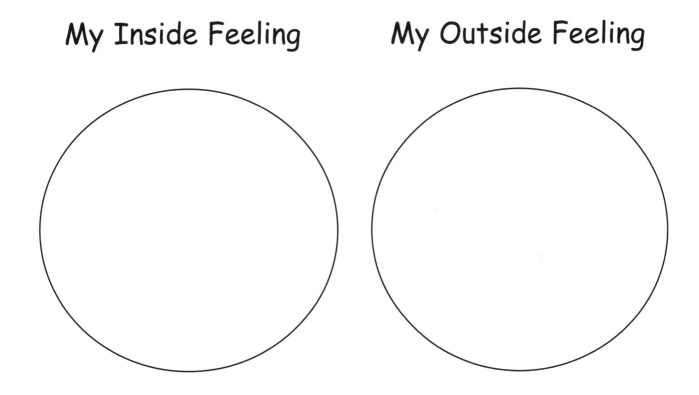

My Inside Feeling   My Outside Feeling

It doesn't feel good when your "inside" feelings don't match your "outside" feelings. You can learn to express all feelings in ways that are O.K.—even fear, hurt, and frustration.

Something I did when I was angry got me in big trouble.

(Draw what you did.)

(Draw what happened.)

Angry behavior can hurt people and things.

I did something embarrassing when I was angry.

(Draw a picture of why you were angry.)

(Draw what you did.)

People can do foolish things when they are angry.

Sometimes my friends get angry and do dumb things, and I don't want to be with them.

(Draw some things your friends do when they are angry.)

Angry behavior can make people unpopular, and it can even ruin friendships.

When people get angry, their brains don't work right and they can make poor choices. If they lose control, they may hurt someone or do something they will regret. If they hold their anger inside, it can turn into pain, illness, or depression. When I get angry, I . . .

(Draw what you do when you get angry.)

Poor anger management can waste time and energy. Other people avoid angry people.

I am sorry about something I did when I was angry.

(Draw a picture of what happened.)

You can learn to manage your anger so it does not control your behavior.

It is hard to fight fair when I am fighting mad.
But some behaviors cause bigger problems.

(Circle the things you do.)

1. Screaming or throwing temper tantrums.
2. Breaking things.
3. Being mean.
4. Hitting or biting.
5. Name calling or putdowns.
6. Lying or blaming someone else.
7. Threatening.
8. Teasing.
9. Other: _____
10. Other: _____

Learn how to attack the problem and not the
other person.

Thoughts and beliefs trigger feelings. But sometimes, what I think or believe isn't true.

(Draw something that made you angry until you learned it wasn't true.)

If you change what you think or believe, your feelings and behaviors will change. Let's say someone pushes you down at recess. If you tell yourself they did it on purpose, you might feel so angry that you want to push back. But if you tell yourself it could have been an accident, you wouldn't feel as angry.

I can learn to relax when I feel myself getting angry.

1. I can count to 10.
2. I can repeat to myself: "I am upset, but I can handle this."
3. I can relax my body like a rag doll. I can breathe out and let go of my anger. I can breathe in strength and control.
4. I can leave an angry situation and go listen to calm music while I draw or paint.
5. I can: _____

_____

_____

_____

Calming thoughts and deep breathing can help you relax and make better choices.

Things will not always go my way. I will not always get what I want.

(Draw or write what you will do to calm yourself.)

You cannot always control what happens to you, but you can control what you think and what you do.

I can distract myself by thinking of a happy time when everything seemed good. I can remember all the happy sounds and smells and feelings.

(Draw a time you felt proud and happy.)

You can bring this picture to your mind when you begin to feel angry. This will give you time to cool down.

Some people think that anger is bad, or that nice people don't get angry. They might even be afraid of making others angry. It's not easy, but it's important to let angry feelings out in healthy ways. Otherwise, my body could get sick.

(Use a crayon to scribble where you get aches and pains.)

Look on page 10 to see if these are the same places you feel your anger.

It's hard to feel good when angry feelings are kept inside.

There are people or things I feel angry about.

(Draw some pictures about them.)

Scribble your anger on an old newspaper with a red crayon. Scrunch the newspaper into a ball. Push your anger into the ball and out of your mind. This will not hurt anyone and you will feel better. Throw the ball away.

I can put my anger into words to say what I am thinking and feeling.

1. I will slow down and count to 10.
2. I won't say the first thing I think.
3. I will think about what I need.
4. I will think about what is really causing my anger.
5. I will stay calm.
6. I will identify my feelings and say:
   "I feel _____
   when you _____
   because _____.
   I need _____."
   Or I will say:
   "I do not like that!"
   "Stop that."
   "Leave me alone."

It is important to use "I" instead of "you."

When my anger builds up at people and I cannot tell them, I can imagine them in a silly way.

(Draw someone in a silly costume.)

You can decide what to do with your anger.

If I do not express my anger, I may become resentful or depressed. There are many healthy ways to express anger.

(Check ✓ the ones you do.)

____ Write feelings on a piece of paper, then tear it up.

____ Draw an angry picture, then scribble it out.

____ Squeeze or pound clay.

____ Talk to pets or stuffed animals.

____ Share feelings with caring adults.

____ Play sports or bounce a ball.

____ Listen to soothing and relaxing music.

____ Make a pretend phone call.

____ Tell problems to a good friend.

____ Shout into a pillow.

____ Have a good cry in a safe place.

It is not O.K. to hurt yourself or others when you are angry.

I know some people who get very angry.

(Draw a picture of them and how they show their anger.)

It is natural for family and friends to feel angry at each other. But the way they show their anger makes a big difference.

Sometimes I think it is my fault when others get angry, so I do something to try to change their feelings.

(Draw a picture of what you do.)

You are not responsible for the feelings of others. You are only responsible for your own feelings and behaviors.

When people have been frightened by another person's anger, they feel powerless. They might act or talk mean to someone else to feel more powerful.

(Draw a picture of a bully.)

Learning anger management is true power. Brain power can be stronger than muscle power.

Some children—and adults—like to bully those who are smaller and weaker than they are.

(If this has happened to you, draw a picture of what happened and how you felt.)

Bullies are people who have poor anger-management skills. Sometimes they pick on people who do not look confident. Victims must learn to stand up for themselves or seek adult help.

Some people get picked on because they look and feel weak.

(Draw a picture of how they sit or stand.)

Confident people often avoid bullies because they sit and walk tall. They feel good about themselves. You can, too.

I am learning to manage my anger, and I feel proud and confident.

(Draw a picture of yourself.)

Congratulations! Give yourself a gold star. You are a winner!